35 Caribbean & West Indian Recipes for Home

By: Kelly Johnson

Table of Contents

Appetizers:

Thai Fresh Spring Rolls:
- Fresh vegetables, herbs, and sometimes shrimp or chicken wrapped in rice paper, served with peanut or hoisin sauce.

Malaysian Satay Skewers:
- Grilled skewers of marinated meat (often chicken or beef) served with a flavorful peanut sauce.

Indonesian Rendang Puffs:
- Mini pastry puffs filled with rendang, a rich and aromatic coconut beef stew.

Vietnamese Banh Xeo (Sizzling Pancakes):
- Crispy rice flour pancakes filled with shrimp, pork, bean sprouts, and herbs.

Burmese Tea Leaf Salad (Laphet Thoke):
- A unique salad with fermented tea leaves, crunchy nuts, seeds, and various toppings.

Main Courses:

Thai Green Curry with Chicken:
- A fragrant and creamy curry made with green curry paste, coconut milk, and chicken.

Singaporean Chili Crab:
- Mud crabs stir-fried in a spicy, sweet, and tangy chili sauce.

Filipino Adobo Chicken:
- Chicken braised in a mixture of soy sauce, vinegar, garlic, and bay leaves.

Cambodian Fish Amok:
- Fish steamed in a coconut milk and curry paste mixture, often served in banana leaves.

Lao Larb Gai (Minced Chicken Salad):
- A spicy and tangy minced chicken salad with herbs and toasted rice powder.

Malaysian Nasi Lemak:

- Fragrant coconut rice served with anchovies, peanuts, boiled eggs, and sambal.

Vietnamese Pho Bo (Beef Noodle Soup):
- A comforting soup with beef, rice noodles, and aromatic spices.

Pad Thai:
- A classic Thai stir-fried noodle dish with a perfect balance of sweet, sour, and savory flavors. It typically includes rice noodles, shrimp, tofu or chicken, bean sprouts, peanuts, and lime.

Nasi Goreng:
- Indonesian fried rice seasoned with kecap manis (sweet soy sauce), shallots, garlic, tamarind, and chilli, and accompanied by ingredients like fried eggs, prawns, and chicken.

Green Curry Chicken (Gaeng Keow Wan Gai):
- A Thai curry dish made with green curry paste, coconut milk, chicken, and a variety of vegetables. It's known for its vibrant green color and rich, aromatic flavor.

Chicken Adobo:
- A Filipino dish featuring chicken marinated and cooked in a mixture of soy sauce, vinegar, garlic, and bay leaves until tender. It's often served with steamed rice.

Beef Rendang:
- An Indonesian and Malaysian dry curry that features slow-cooked beef in coconut milk and a flavorful spice paste. The result is tender, caramelized beef with a rich and aromatic sauce.

Tom Yum Goong:
- A popular Thai hot and sour soup with shrimp. It typically includes ingredients like lemongrass, kaffir lime leaves, galangal, lime juice, and fish sauce.

Laksa:
- A spicy noodle soup that's a fusion of Chinese and Malay flavors. There are different variations, but it often includes coconut milk, curry spices, prawns, and sometimes chicken or tofu.

Banh Mi Sandwich:
- A harmonious fusion of flavors and textures, featuring a crisp baguette enveloping succulent grilled protein, tangy pickled vegetables, spicy Sriracha mayo, and fresh herbs for a delightful culinary journey.

Seafood Dishes:

Thai Basil Shrimp Stir-Fry:
- Shrimp stir-fried with Thai basil, chili, and garlic.

Indonesian Grilled Fish (Ikan Bakar):
- Fish marinated in a spicy paste and grilled to perfection.

Burmese Mohinga (Fish Soup):
- A fish-based soup with rice noodles, lemongrass, and a variety of toppings.

Vegetarian Delights:

Indian Vegetable Biryani:
- Fragrant basmati rice cooked with mixed vegetables and aromatic spices.

Thai Green Papaya Salad (Som Tum):
- Shredded green papaya mixed with lime, chili, fish sauce, and peanuts.

Vietnamese Vegan Pho Chay:
- A plant-based version of the classic Vietnamese pho.

Side Dishes:

Indonesian Gado Gado:
- A mixed vegetable salad with peanut sauce dressing.

Cambodian Pickled Vegetables (Tuk Meric):
- Tangy and spicy pickled vegetables served as a side dish.

Desserts:

Thai Mango Sticky Rice (Khao Niew Mamuang):
- Sweet sticky rice topped with ripe mango slices and coconut milk.

Malaysian Kuih Dadar (Pandan Crepes):
- Pandan-flavored crepes filled with sweet coconut and palm sugar.

Filipino Halo-Halo:
- A colorful and refreshing dessert with shaved ice, various fruits, and sweet beans.

Vietnamese Coffee Ice Cream:

- Indulge in a rich and creamy frozen delight featuring the bold flavors of strong Vietnamese coffee, with a decadent coffee swirl for a delightful frozen treat.

Beverages:

Vietnamese Iced Coffee (Ca Phe Sua Da):
- Strong Vietnamese coffee with condensed milk, served over ice.

Thai Iced Tea (Cha Yen):
- Sweet and creamy Thai tea served cold with condensed milk.

Indonesian Avocado Shake (Es Alpukat):
- A creamy and sweet shake made with ripe avocados and condensed milk.

Appetizers:

Thai Fresh Spring Rolls:

Ingredients:

For the Spring Rolls:

- 8 rice paper wrappers
- 1 cup cooked and peeled shrimp, halved (or shredded cooked chicken for a non-seafood version)
- 2 cups vermicelli rice noodles, cooked
- 1 cucumber, julienned
- 1 carrot, julienned
- 1 bell pepper, thinly sliced
- Fresh cilantro leaves
- Fresh mint leaves
- Lettuce leaves (such as butter or iceberg)
- Spring onion, thinly sliced

For the Dipping Sauce:

- 1/4 cup hoisin sauce
- 2 tablespoons peanut butter
- 2 tablespoons soy sauce
- 1 tablespoon rice vinegar
- 1 teaspoon sesame oil
- Water (to thin, if needed)

Instructions:

Prepare Ingredients:
- Cook the vermicelli rice noodles according to package instructions and let them cool.
- Prepare all the vegetables, herbs, and protein.

Soak Rice Paper Wrappers:
- Fill a shallow dish with warm water. Dip one rice paper wrapper into the water for about 5-10 seconds until it softens.

Assemble the Spring Rolls:
- Lay the softened rice paper on a clean surface.
- On one edge of the wrapper, place a small amount of shrimp or chicken, a handful of vermicelli noodles, cucumber, carrot, bell pepper, cilantro, mint, lettuce, and spring onion.

Roll the Spring Rolls:
- Fold the sides of the rice paper over the filling and then tightly roll from the bottom to the top, similar to rolling a burrito.

Repeat:
- Repeat the process until all ingredients are used.

Prepare Dipping Sauce:
- In a small bowl, whisk together hoisin sauce, peanut butter, soy sauce, rice vinegar, and sesame oil until well combined. If the sauce is too thick, you can add water to achieve the desired consistency.

Serve:
- Serve the Thai Fresh Spring Rolls with the dipping sauce on the side.

Enjoy these Thai Fresh Spring Rolls as a light and refreshing appetizer or as a healthy meal. The combination of fresh vegetables, herbs, and protein wrapped in rice paper is a delightful and flavorful experience.

Malaysian Satay Skewers with Peanut Sauce:

Ingredients:

For the Satay Marinade:

- 1 kg chicken or beef, cut into bite-sized pieces
- 1 onion, finely grated
- 3 cloves garlic, minced
- 1 thumb-sized ginger, grated
- 2 tablespoons lemongrass, finely chopped
- 2 tablespoons soy sauce
- 2 tablespoons vegetable oil
- 1 tablespoon turmeric powder
- 1 tablespoon coriander powder
- 1 teaspoon cumin powder
- 1 teaspoon chili powder (adjust to taste)
- Salt and pepper to taste

For the Peanut Sauce:

- 1 cup unsweetened peanut butter
- 1/2 cup coconut milk
- 2 tablespoons soy sauce
- 2 tablespoons brown sugar
- 1 tablespoon tamarind paste
- 2 cloves garlic, minced
- 1 teaspoon ginger, grated
- 1 teaspoon chili paste (adjust to taste)
- Water (to adjust consistency)
- Lime wedges (for serving)

For Skewers:

- Bamboo skewers, soaked in water for at least 30 minutes

Instructions:

For the Satay Skewers:

Prepare Marinade:
- In a bowl, combine grated onion, minced garlic, grated ginger, chopped lemongrass, soy sauce, vegetable oil, turmeric powder, coriander powder, cumin powder, chili powder, salt, and pepper. Mix well to form the marinade.

Marinate Meat:
- Coat the chicken or beef pieces in the marinade, ensuring they are well-covered. Allow the meat to marinate for at least 2 hours or overnight in the refrigerator.

Skewer the Meat:
- Thread the marinated meat onto soaked bamboo skewers.

Grill:
- Grill the skewers on a preheated barbecue or grill pan until the meat is cooked through and has a nice char on the edges.

For the Peanut Sauce:

Prepare Peanut Sauce:
- In a saucepan over medium heat, combine peanut butter, coconut milk, soy sauce, brown sugar, tamarind paste, minced garlic, grated ginger, and chili paste. Stir continuously until well combined.

Adjust Consistency:
- If the sauce is too thick, add water gradually until you reach the desired consistency. Continue stirring.

Simmer:
- Let the sauce simmer for a few minutes to allow the flavors to meld. Adjust the seasoning if needed.

Serve:

Presentation:
- Arrange the grilled satay skewers on a serving platter.

Drizzle Sauce:
- Drizzle the peanut sauce over the skewers or serve it on the side for dipping.

Garnish:
- Garnish with chopped peanuts and serve with lime wedges.

Enjoy these Malaysian Satay Skewers with Peanut Sauce as a flavorful and satisfying appetizer or main dish. The combination of the well-marinated grilled meat and the rich peanut sauce creates a delicious and authentic Malaysian experience.

Indonesian Rendang Puffs:

Ingredients:

For Rendang Filling:

- 500g beef, thinly sliced
- 1 can (400ml) coconut milk
- 2 stalks lemongrass, bruised
- 4 kaffir lime leaves
- 3 tablespoons rendang curry paste (store-bought or homemade)
- 2 tablespoons tamarind paste
- 2 tablespoons palm sugar or brown sugar
- 1 tablespoon tamarind paste
- Salt to taste
- Cooking oil

For Puff Pastry:

- Store-bought puff pastry sheets (or homemade if preferred)

Instructions:

For Rendang Filling:

Cook Beef:
- In a pan, heat cooking oil over medium heat. Add the rendang curry paste and cook until fragrant.

Add Beef:
- Add the thinly sliced beef to the pan and cook until it is browned on all sides.

Coconut Milk Mixture:
- Pour in the coconut milk, lemongrass, kaffir lime leaves, tamarind paste, palm sugar, and salt. Stir well to combine.

Simmer:
- Bring the mixture to a boil, then reduce the heat to low and let it simmer for 2-3 hours or until the beef is tender and the sauce has thickened. Stir occasionally to prevent sticking.

Adjust Seasoning:

- Adjust the seasoning with additional salt, sugar, or tamarind paste if needed. The rendang should have a rich, aromatic, and slightly sweet flavor.

Remove Lemongrass and Lime Leaves:
- Once the rendang is ready, remove the lemongrass stalks and kaffir lime leaves. Allow the mixture to cool.

For Puff Pastry:

Preheat Oven:
- Preheat your oven according to the instructions on the puff pastry package.

Prepare Pastry Sheets:
- Roll out the puff pastry sheets on a lightly floured surface. Cut the sheets into squares or circles, depending on your preference and the size of the pastry puffs you want.

Fill Pastry:
- Place a spoonful of the cooled rendang filling in the center of each pastry square or circle.

Seal Pastry:
- Fold the pastry over the filling to create a triangle or half-circle shape. Use a fork to press the edges and seal the pastry.

Bake:
- Arrange the filled pastries on a baking sheet and bake according to the puff pastry package instructions or until the pastry is golden brown and puffed up.

Serve:
- Once baked, let the rendang puffs cool for a few minutes before serving.

Enjoy these Indonesian Rendang Puffs as a delightful appetizer or snack, showcasing the rich and aromatic flavors of traditional rendang in a convenient pastry form.

Vietnamese Banh Xeo (Sizzling Pancakes):

Ingredients:

For the Pancake Batter:

- 1 cup rice flour
- 1 cup coconut milk
- 1 cup water
- 1/2 teaspoon turmeric powder
- 1/2 teaspoon salt
- 1/2 teaspoon sugar
- 1/2 teaspoon ground black pepper
- 2 green onions, finely chopped

For the Filling:

- 200g shrimp, peeled and deveined
- 150g pork belly or pork shoulder, thinly sliced
- 1 cup bean sprouts
- 1 onion, thinly sliced
- Fresh herbs (cilantro, mint, and basil)
- Lettuce leaves

For the Dipping Sauce:

- 3 tablespoons fish sauce
- 2 tablespoons rice vinegar
- 1 tablespoon sugar
- 1/2 cup water
- 1 garlic clove, minced
- 1 red chili, finely chopped (optional)

Instructions:

For the Pancake Batter:

    Prepare Batter:

- In a bowl, whisk together rice flour, coconut milk, water, turmeric powder, salt, sugar, ground black pepper, and chopped green onions. Let the batter rest for at least 30 minutes.

For the Filling:

Cook Shrimp and Pork:
- In a pan, cook the shrimp and pork slices until they are fully cooked. Set aside.

Prepare Vegetables:
- Slice the onion thinly and wash the bean sprouts and fresh herbs. Arrange lettuce leaves on a serving plate.

For Cooking Banh Xeo:

Heat Pan:
- Heat a non-stick pan or a well-seasoned cast-iron skillet over medium-high heat.

Add Batter:
- Pour a ladle of the pancake batter into the hot pan, swirling it to coat the bottom evenly. The batter should sizzle as it hits the pan.

Add Filling:
- Quickly add some cooked shrimp, pork slices, sliced onions, and bean sprouts to one side of the pancake.

Fold and Serve:
- Allow the pancake to cook until the edges become crispy. Fold the other half of the pancake over the filling, creating a half-moon shape. Slide it onto a serving plate with lettuce leaves.

For Dipping Sauce:

Prepare Dipping Sauce:
- In a bowl, mix fish sauce, rice vinegar, sugar, water, minced garlic, and chopped red chili (if using). Stir until the sugar dissolves.

Serve:
- Serve the Banh Xeo hot with fresh herbs and lettuce leaves for wrapping. Dip each bite into the tangy dipping sauce.

Enjoy these Vietnamese Banh Xeo as a delicious and interactive meal. The combination of crispy pancakes, flavorful fillings, and fresh herbs creates a delightful eating experience.

Burmese Tea Leaf Salad (Laphet Thoke):

Ingredients:

For Fermented Tea Leaves:

- 1 cup fermented tea leaves (available in Asian grocery stores)
- 2 tablespoons peanut oil
- 1 tablespoon fish sauce
- 1 tablespoon soy sauce
- 1 teaspoon shrimp paste (optional)
- 1 teaspoon sugar
- 1 clove garlic, minced

For Salad Assembly:

- 3 cups mixed salad greens (lettuce, spinach, or other leafy greens)
- 1 cup shredded cabbage
- 1/2 cup cherry tomatoes, halved
- 1/4 cup roasted peanuts, chopped
- 1/4 cup toasted sesame seeds
- 1/4 cup fried garlic slices
- 2 tablespoons fried yellow split peas (optional)
- 1 tablespoon dried shrimp, toasted (optional)

For Dressing:

- 2 tablespoons peanut oil
- 1 tablespoon lime juice
- 1 tablespoon fish sauce
- 1 teaspoon soy sauce
- 1 teaspoon honey or palm sugar
- 1 clove garlic, minced
- 1 red chili, finely chopped (optional)

Instructions:

For Fermented Tea Leaves:

Prepare Tea Leaves:
- Soak the fermented tea leaves in water for about 15 minutes to soften them. Drain and set aside.

Make Dressing:
- In a bowl, whisk together peanut oil, fish sauce, soy sauce, shrimp paste (if using), sugar, and minced garlic. Add the drained tea leaves and mix well.

For Salad Assembly:

Prepare Salad Ingredients:
- In a large salad bowl, combine mixed salad greens, shredded cabbage, cherry tomatoes, chopped peanuts, toasted sesame seeds, fried garlic slices, fried yellow split peas (if using), and toasted dried shrimp (if using).

Add Tea Leaves:
- Pour the tea leaf dressing over the salad ingredients. Toss everything together until well combined.

For Dressing:

Prepare Dressing:
- In a small bowl, whisk together peanut oil, lime juice, fish sauce, soy sauce, honey or palm sugar, minced garlic, and chopped red chili (if using).

Dress the Salad:
- Pour the dressing over the assembled salad and toss gently to coat the ingredients with the dressing.

Serve:
- Garnish with additional peanuts, sesame seeds, and fried garlic if desired. Serve the Burmese Tea Leaf Salad immediately.

Enjoy the unique and flavorful taste of Burmese Tea Leaf Salad (Laphet Thoke) with its combination of fermented tea leaves, crunchy nuts, and a variety of toppings. It's a refreshing and distinctive salad that brings a taste of Myanmar to your table.

Main Courses:

Thai Green Curry with Chicken:

Ingredients:

For Green Curry Paste:

- 2 green chili peppers, chopped
- 1 shallot, chopped
- 3 cloves garlic, minced
- 1 lemongrass stalk, chopped (white part only)
- 1 thumb-sized galangal or ginger, sliced
- 1 kaffir lime zest or 1 teaspoon lime zest
- 1 teaspoon coriander seeds, toasted
- 1/2 teaspoon cumin seeds, toasted
- 1/2 teaspoon white pepper
- 1 tablespoon shrimp paste (optional, for non-vegetarian version)

For Green Curry:

- 1 pound chicken breast or thighs, cut into bite-sized pieces
- 2 tablespoons green curry paste (store-bought or homemade)
- 1 can (400ml) coconut milk
- 1 cup chicken broth
- 1 cup mixed vegetables (such as bamboo shoots, bell peppers, and Thai eggplant)
- 2 tablespoons fish sauce (adjust to taste)
- 1 tablespoon soy sauce
- 1 tablespoon palm sugar or brown sugar
- Fresh Thai basil leaves for garnish
- Red chili slices for garnish (optional)

Instructions:

For Green Curry Paste:

Blend Ingredients:
- In a blender or food processor, combine green chili peppers, shallot, garlic, lemongrass, galangal or ginger, kaffir lime zest, toasted coriander seeds, toasted cumin seeds, white pepper, and shrimp paste (if using). Blend until it forms a smooth paste.

For Green Curry:

Prepare Chicken:
- In a pot or deep pan, heat a bit of oil over medium heat. Add the green curry paste and sauté for a few minutes until it becomes aromatic.

Cook Chicken:
- Add the chicken pieces to the pot and cook until they are no longer pink on the outside.

Add Coconut Milk and Broth:
- Pour in the coconut milk and chicken broth. Bring the mixture to a gentle simmer.

Add Vegetables:
- Add the mixed vegetables to the pot. Simmer until the chicken is fully cooked and the vegetables are tender.

Season the Curry:
- Season the curry with fish sauce, soy sauce, and palm sugar. Adjust the seasoning according to your taste preferences.

Simmer:
- Let the curry simmer for an additional 5-10 minutes to allow the flavors to meld.

Garnish and Serve:
- Garnish the Thai Green Curry with fresh Thai basil leaves and red chili slices (if using). Serve the curry over steamed jasmine rice.

Enjoy the fragrant and creamy goodness of Thai Green Curry with Chicken, a classic Thai dish that brings together a harmonious blend of aromatic herbs and spices.

Singaporean Chili Crab:

Ingredients:

For Chili Sauce:

- 10 red chili peppers, seeds removed and chopped
- 5 bird's eye chili peppers, chopped (adjust for spice level)
- 4 cloves garlic, minced
- 2 tablespoons ginger, minced
- 1/2 cup tomato ketchup
- 1/4 cup sweet chili sauce
- 2 tablespoons soy sauce
- 2 tablespoons oyster sauce
- 1 tablespoon brown sugar
- 1 tablespoon tamarind paste
- 1 cup water

For Crab:

- 2 large mud crabs, cleaned and cut into pieces
- 2 tablespoons vegetable oil
- 1 onion, finely chopped
- 2 spring onions, chopped (separate white and green parts)
- 1 egg, beaten
- Fresh cilantro leaves for garnish
- Lime wedges for serving

Instructions:

For Chili Sauce:

   Blend Ingredients:
   - In a blender, combine red chili peppers, bird's eye chili peppers, minced garlic, minced ginger, tomato ketchup, sweet chili sauce, soy sauce, oyster

sauce, brown sugar, tamarind paste, and water. Blend until you get a smooth sauce.

For Chili Crab:

Prepare Crabs:
- Clean the mud crabs, remove the top shell, and cut them into pieces.

Stir-Fry Crab:
- In a wok or large pan, heat vegetable oil over medium-high heat. Add the chopped onion and the white parts of the spring onions. Stir-fry until the onions are translucent.

Add Chili Sauce:
- Pour in the prepared chili sauce and bring it to a simmer.

Cook Crab:
- Add the crab pieces to the wok, coating them in the chili sauce. Cover and let it cook for about 10-15 minutes, or until the crab is cooked through. Stir occasionally to ensure even cooking.

Finish with Egg:
- Once the crab is almost cooked, pour the beaten egg over the crab and sauce. Gently stir to combine, allowing the egg to create a silky texture in the sauce.

Garnish and Serve:
- Garnish with the green parts of the spring onions and fresh cilantro leaves.

Serve with Lime:
- Serve the Singaporean Chili Crab hot, with lime wedges on the side.

Enjoy the delightful and flavorful Singaporean Chili Crab, a famous and beloved dish known for its spicy, sweet, and tangy sauce that perfectly complements the succulent crab meat. Serve it with steamed rice or crusty bread to soak up the delicious sauce.

Filipino Adobo Chicken:

Ingredients:

- 2 pounds chicken, cut into serving pieces
- 1 onion, peeled and sliced thinly
- 1 head garlic, peeled and minced
- 1/2 cup soy sauce
- 1/4 cup vinegar (white or cane vinegar)
- 1 teaspoon black peppercorns, crushed
- 3 bay leaves
- 1 cup water
- 2 tablespoons cooking oil

Instructions:

Marinate Chicken:
- In a large bowl, combine chicken, soy sauce, vinegar, minced garlic, crushed black peppercorns, and bay leaves. Massage the marinade into the chicken pieces. Let it marinate for at least 30 minutes to an hour, or overnight in the refrigerator for a more intense flavor.

Sauté Onions:
- In a wide, heavy-bottomed pan, heat cooking oil over medium heat. Add the sliced onions and sauté until they become soft and translucent.

Brown Chicken:
- Add the marinated chicken to the pan. Brown the chicken pieces on all sides, stirring occasionally.

Add Marinade and Water:
- Pour in the remaining marinade, including the garlic and bay leaves. Add water to the pan. Allow it to come to a boil.

Simmer:
- Once boiling, reduce the heat to a simmer. Cover the pan and let it cook for about 30-40 minutes or until the chicken is tender and the flavors have melded. Stir occasionally to ensure even cooking.

Adjust Seasoning:
- Taste the adobo and adjust the seasoning with more soy sauce, vinegar, or pepper according to your preference.

Serve:

- Serve the Filipino Adobo Chicken over steamed rice. Garnish with sliced green onions or fresh cilantro if desired.

Enjoy the savory and tangy flavors of Filipino Adobo Chicken, a classic and beloved dish that showcases the delicious combination of soy sauce, vinegar, and aromatic spices. It's a comforting and satisfying meal that pairs perfectly with steamed rice.

Cambodian Fish Amok:

Ingredients:

For Fish Marinade:

- 1 pound white fish fillets, cut into bite-sized pieces
- 1 tablespoon fish sauce
- 1 tablespoon lime juice

For Amok Paste:

- 2 stalks lemongrass, finely chopped (white part only)
- 4 kaffir lime leaves, finely chopped
- 2 shallots, finely chopped
- 4 cloves garlic, minced
- 1 thumb-sized piece of galangal or ginger, grated
- 2 red chili peppers, seeds removed and chopped
- 1 teaspoon ground turmeric
- 1 teaspoon shrimp paste (optional)
- 1 tablespoon vegetable oil

For Amok Sauce:

- 1 can (400ml) coconut milk
- 2 tablespoons fish sauce
- 1 tablespoon palm sugar or brown sugar

Additional Ingredients:

- Banana leaves (for wrapping and serving)
- Fresh cilantro leaves for garnish

Instructions:

For Fish Marinade:

Marinate Fish:
- In a bowl, combine fish fillets with fish sauce and lime juice. Let it marinate for at least 15-30 minutes.

For Amok Paste:

Prepare Amok Paste:
- In a blender or mortar and pestle, blend lemongrass, kaffir lime leaves, shallots, garlic, galangal or ginger, red chili peppers, ground turmeric, and shrimp paste (if using) until it forms a smooth paste.

Sauté Paste:
- Heat vegetable oil in a pan and sauté the amok paste over medium heat for about 5-7 minutes until fragrant.

For Amok Sauce:

Add Coconut Milk:
- Pour in coconut milk, fish sauce, and palm sugar to the sautéed amok paste. Stir well and let it simmer for another 5 minutes.

Assembly and Cooking:

Prepare Banana Leaves:
- Cut banana leaves into rectangles, and quickly pass them over an open flame to soften them (this makes them pliable for wrapping).

Form Banana Leaf Cups:
- Create small cups using the banana leaves by folding and securing with toothpicks or kitchen twine.

Layer Fish and Sauce:
- Place a portion of marinated fish in each banana leaf cup, and pour the amok sauce over the fish.

Steam:
- Steam the banana leaf cups with the fish and sauce for about 15-20 minutes or until the fish is cooked through.

Garnish:
- Garnish with fresh cilantro leaves.

Serve:

- Serve the Cambodian Fish Amok hot in the banana leaf cups. It's traditionally served with rice.

Enjoy the rich and aromatic flavors of Cambodian Fish Amok, a dish that beautifully showcases the combination of coconut milk, curry paste, and tender fish, all steamed to perfection in banana leaves.

Lao Larb Gai (Minced Chicken Salad):

Ingredients:

For Larb:

- 1 pound ground chicken
- 2 tablespoons cooking oil
- 2 tablespoons fish sauce
- 3 tablespoons lime juice
- 1 tablespoon soy sauce
- 1 tablespoon sugar
- 1/2 teaspoon chili flakes (adjust to taste)
- 2 shallots, finely chopped
- 3 green onions, chopped
- 2 tablespoons fresh mint leaves, chopped
- 2 tablespoons fresh cilantro leaves, chopped
- 1 tablespoon toasted rice powder (see instructions below)

For Toasted Rice Powder:

- 1/4 cup glutinous rice (sticky rice)

For Serving:

- Lettuce leaves (for wrapping)
- Fresh herbs (mint, cilantro, basil)
- Sliced cucumber and lime wedges (optional)

Instructions:

For Larb:

    Cook Ground Chicken:
- In a skillet, heat cooking oil over medium heat. Add ground chicken and cook until fully browned and cooked through.

    Make Larb Sauce:
- In a bowl, mix fish sauce, lime juice, soy sauce, sugar, and chili flakes. Adjust the seasoning to your taste.

    Combine Ingredients:

- In a large bowl, combine the cooked ground chicken, chopped shallots, green onions, mint leaves, and cilantro leaves.

Add Sauce:
- Pour the larb sauce over the mixture and toss everything together until well combined.

Sprinkle with Toasted Rice Powder:
- Sprinkle toasted rice powder over the larb mixture. Toss again to incorporate the rice powder.

For Toasted Rice Powder:

Toast Rice:
- In a dry pan, toast glutinous rice over medium heat until golden brown. Stir constantly to prevent burning.

Grind into Powder:
- Once toasted, let the rice cool and then grind it into a coarse powder using a mortar and pestle or a spice grinder.

For Serving:

Prepare Lettuce Cups:
- Wash and separate lettuce leaves to use as cups for the larb.

Serve:
- Spoon the larb mixture into the lettuce cups. Garnish with fresh herbs and serve with sliced cucumber and lime wedges if desired.

Lao Larb Gai is best enjoyed by assembling the lettuce cups with the flavorful minced chicken mixture, creating a delicious and refreshing bite. The combination of herbs, spices, and the unique toasted rice powder adds depth and texture to this traditional Lao dish.

Malaysian Nasi Lemak:

Ingredients:

For Coconut Rice:

- 2 cups jasmine rice
- 1 cup coconut milk
- 1 cup water
- 2 pandan leaves (optional)
- 1/2 teaspoon salt

For Sambal (Chili Paste):

- 10 dried red chilies, soaked in hot water
- 4 shallots
- 3 cloves garlic
- 1 inch ginger
- 2 tablespoons tamarind paste
- 2 tablespoons palm sugar or brown sugar
- 1 teaspoon salt

For Accompaniments:

- Hard-boiled eggs, halved
- Fried anchovies
- Roasted peanuts
- Sliced cucumber

Instructions:

For Coconut Rice:

Rinse and Soak Rice:
- Rinse the jasmine rice under cold water until the water runs clear. Soak the rice in water for 30 minutes, then drain.

Cook Rice:
- In a rice cooker or pot, combine the soaked rice, coconut milk, water, pandan leaves (if using), and salt. Cook the rice according to your rice cooker's instructions or until done.

Fluff Rice:
- Once cooked, fluff the rice with a fork to separate the grains. Remove pandan leaves.

For Sambal (Chili Paste):

Prepare Sambal Paste:
- In a blender, blend soaked dried chilies, shallots, garlic, and ginger into a smooth paste.

Cook Sambal:
- Heat a bit of oil in a pan and sauté the blended paste until fragrant. Add tamarind paste, palm sugar, and salt. Cook until the sambal thickens. Adjust sweetness and saltiness to your liking.

For Serving:

Assemble Nasi Lemak:
- Serve the coconut rice with a side of sambal, hard-boiled eggs, fried anchovies, roasted peanuts, and sliced cucumber.

Enjoy:
- Mix the sambal with the coconut rice and pair it with the various accompaniments. Enjoy the flavorful Malaysian Nasi Lemak!

Nasi Lemak is a beloved Malaysian dish known for its fragrant coconut rice and delicious sambal. Customize your plate with the accompaniments to suit your taste, and savor the rich and aromatic flavors that make this dish a true Malaysian delight.

Vietnamese Pho Bo (Beef Noodle Soup):

Ingredients:

For Broth:

- 2 large onions, halved
- 1 ginger piece (about 3 inches), sliced
- 3-4 lbs beef bones (marrow and knuckle bones)
- 1 lb beef brisket or flank
- 5 star anise
- 5 whole cloves
- 1 cinnamon stick
- 1 cardamom pod
- 1 tablespoon coriander seeds
- 1 tablespoon salt
- 2 tablespoons fish sauce
- 1 tablespoon sugar
- 1 tablespoon rock sugar (or regular sugar)

For Serving:

- Flat rice noodles (bánh phở)
- Thinly sliced raw beef (eye of round or sirloin)
- Fresh herbs: cilantro, Thai basil, mint
- Bean sprouts
- Lime wedges
- Sliced chili (optional)
- Hoisin sauce and Sriracha (optional)

Instructions:

For Broth:

Char Onions and Ginger:

- Char the halved onions and sliced ginger under a broiler or over an open flame until they are slightly blackened.

Parboil Beef Bones:
- Bring a large pot of water to a boil. Add beef bones and boil vigorously for 10 minutes. Discard the water, clean the bones, and rinse the pot.

Simmer Broth:
- Fill the cleaned pot with about 4 quarts of water. Add the parboiled beef bones, charred onions, charred ginger, star anise, cloves, cinnamon stick, cardamom pod, coriander seeds, salt, fish sauce, sugar, and rock sugar. Bring to a boil.

Skim the Surface:
- Once boiling, reduce heat to a simmer. Skim any foam and impurities that rise to the surface.

Cook Brisket or Flank:
- Add the beef brisket or flank to the simmering broth. Cook until it's just done, about 20-30 minutes. Remove and slice thinly.

Strain Broth:
- After simmering for at least 1.5 to 2 hours, strain the broth through a fine mesh strainer. Adjust seasoning if needed.

For Serving:

Prepare Rice Noodles:
- Cook rice noodles according to package instructions. Drain and set aside.

Assemble Pho:
- Divide the cooked rice noodles among serving bowls. Add thinly sliced raw beef on top.

Pour Hot Broth:
- Pour the hot broth over the raw beef and noodles. The hot broth will cook the raw beef slices.

Garnish and Serve:
- Garnish with fresh herbs, bean sprouts, lime wedges, and sliced chili. Serve immediately with hoisin sauce and Sriracha on the side.

Enjoy the comforting and aromatic Vietnamese Pho Bo, a soul-warming bowl of beef noodle soup that's perfect for any occasion. Customize the toppings and condiments to your liking for an authentic and delicious experience.

Pad Thai:

Ingredients:

- 8 oz flat rice noodles
- 1 cup firm tofu, cubed or 1 cup shrimp (peeled and deveined)
- 2 eggs, lightly beaten
- 1 cup bean sprouts
- 1/2 cup chopped green onions
- 1/4 cup crushed peanuts
- Lime wedges for serving

For the Sauce:

- 3 tablespoons tamarind paste
- 2 tablespoons fish sauce (or soy sauce for a vegetarian version)
- 1 tablespoon soy sauce
- 1 tablespoon brown sugar
- 1/2 teaspoon chili flakes (adjust to taste)

Instructions:

Prepare Noodles:
- Soak rice noodles in hot water according to package instructions until they are just tender but still firm. Drain and set aside.

Make the Sauce:
- In a small bowl, whisk together tamarind paste, fish sauce, soy sauce, brown sugar, and chili flakes. Adjust the sweetness and spiciness to your liking.

Cook Protein:
- If using tofu, sauté cubed tofu in a pan until golden brown. If using shrimp, cook until pink and opaque. Push protein to one side of the pan.

Scramble Eggs:
- Pour beaten eggs into the pan on the empty side. Scramble until just set.

Combine Ingredients:
- Add soaked noodles to the pan. Pour the prepared sauce over the noodles. Toss everything together until well combined and heated through.

Add Vegetables:
- Stir in bean sprouts and chopped green onions. Cook for an additional 2-3 minutes until vegetables are slightly tender but still crisp.

Serve:
- Transfer Pad Thai to serving plates. Sprinkle with crushed peanuts and garnish with lime wedges.

Garnish and Enjoy:
- Garnish with extra bean sprouts, green onions, peanuts, and lime wedges. Serve Pad Thai hot and enjoy the explosion of flavors!

Note:

- Customize with your preferred protein and additional veggies like bell peppers or carrots.
- Adjust spice levels by adding more or less chili flakes.
- Pad Thai is traditionally served with a lime wedge, extra peanuts, and chili flakes on the side for diners to adjust according to their taste.

Pad Thai:

Ingredients:

- 8 oz flat rice noodles
- 1 cup firm tofu, cubed or 1 cup shrimp (peeled and deveined)
- 2 eggs, lightly beaten
- 1 cup bean sprouts
- 1/2 cup chopped green onions
- 1/4 cup crushed peanuts
- Lime wedges for serving

For the Sauce:

- 3 tablespoons tamarind paste
- 2 tablespoons fish sauce (or soy sauce for a vegetarian version)
- 1 tablespoon soy sauce
- 1 tablespoon brown sugar
- 1/2 teaspoon chili flakes (adjust to taste)

Instructions:

Prepare Noodles:
- Soak rice noodles in hot water according to package instructions until they are just tender but still firm. Drain and set aside.

Make the Sauce:
- In a small bowl, whisk together tamarind paste, fish sauce, soy sauce, brown sugar, and chili flakes. Adjust the sweetness and spiciness to your liking.

Cook Protein:
- If using tofu, sauté cubed tofu in a pan until golden brown. If using shrimp, cook until pink and opaque. Push protein to one side of the pan.

Scramble Eggs:
- Pour beaten eggs into the pan on the empty side. Scramble until just set.

Combine Ingredients:
- Add soaked noodles to the pan. Pour the prepared sauce over the noodles. Toss everything together until well combined and heated through.

Add Vegetables:
- Stir in bean sprouts and chopped green onions. Cook for an additional 2-3 minutes until vegetables are slightly tender but still crisp.

Serve:
- Transfer Pad Thai to serving plates. Sprinkle with crushed peanuts and garnish with lime wedges.

Garnish and Enjoy:
- Garnish with extra bean sprouts, green onions, peanuts, and lime wedges. Serve Pad Thai hot and enjoy the explosion of flavors!

Note:

- Customize with your preferred protein and additional veggies like bell peppers or carrots.
- Adjust spice levels by adding more or less chili flakes.
- Pad Thai is traditionally served with a lime wedge, extra peanuts, and chili flakes on the side for diners to adjust according to their taste.

Nasi Goreng:

Ingredients:

- 3 cups cooked jasmine rice (preferably day-old)
- 2 tablespoons kecap manis (sweet soy sauce)
- 1 tablespoon soy sauce
- 1 teaspoon tamarind paste
- 2 tablespoons vegetable oil
- 1 onion, finely chopped
- 3 cloves garlic, minced
- 2 red chillies, finely chopped (adjust to taste)
- 1 cup cooked and diced chicken
- 1 cup cooked and peeled prawns
- 2 eggs, fried sunny-side-up
- 2 spring onions, sliced
- Fried shallots for garnish
- Lime wedges for serving

Instructions:

Prepare Ingredients:
- Ensure all ingredients are chopped, cooked, and ready before starting the cooking process.

Mix Sauce:
- In a small bowl, mix kecap manis, soy sauce, and tamarind paste to create the seasoning sauce.

Stir-Fry Aromatics:
- Heat vegetable oil in a wok or large skillet over medium-high heat. Add chopped onions, minced garlic, and chopped red chillies. Stir-fry until fragrant.

Add Protein:
- Add diced chicken and prawns to the wok. Stir-fry until the protein is cooked through and coated with aromatics.

Add Rice:
- Add cooked jasmine rice to the wok. Break up any clumps and ensure the rice is well mixed with other ingredients.

Pour Sauce:

- Pour the prepared sauce over the rice. Continue to stir-fry, ensuring the rice is evenly coated with the sauce.

Finish and Garnish:
- Make a well in the center of the wok and crack the eggs into it. Allow them to fry until the whites are set but the yolks are still runny.

Combine and Season:
- Mix the fried eggs with the rice. Add sliced spring onions and continue to stir-fry until everything is well combined.

Serve:
- Transfer Nasi Goreng to serving plates. Garnish with fried shallots and serve with lime wedges on the side.

Note:

- Feel free to add additional vegetables like peas, carrots, or bell peppers for extra color and texture.
- Adjust the level of spice by adding more or fewer chillies according to your preference.

Green Curry Chicken (Gaeng Keow Wan Gai):

Ingredients:

For the Green Curry Paste:

- 2 green chillies, chopped
- 1 shallot, chopped
- 3 cloves garlic, minced
- 1 lemongrass stalk, sliced
- 1-inch piece of galangal or ginger, grated
- 1 kaffir lime zest (or 1 teaspoon lime zest)
- 1 tablespoon coriander powder
- 1 teaspoon cumin powder
- 1/2 teaspoon black pepper
- 1/2 cup fresh cilantro leaves and stems
- 1/2 cup fresh basil leaves
- 1 tablespoon shrimp paste (optional, for non-vegetarian version)

For the Curry:

- 1 pound chicken thighs, boneless and skinless, sliced
- 2 tablespoons green curry paste
- 1 can (14 oz) coconut milk
- 1 cup chicken broth
- 1 tablespoon fish sauce (or soy sauce for a vegetarian version)
- 1 tablespoon sugar
- 1 cup Thai eggplants, halved (or regular eggplants, diced)
- 1 red bell pepper, sliced
- Fresh basil leaves for garnish
- Cooked jasmine rice for serving

Instructions:

Prepare the Green Curry Paste:

In a blender or food processor, combine all the green curry paste ingredients. Blend until you get a smooth and vibrant green paste.

Make the Green Curry:

In a large pan or wok, heat a tablespoon of oil over medium heat.
Add 2 tablespoons of the green curry paste and sauté for 2-3 minutes until fragrant.
Add sliced chicken and cook until it's no longer pink on the outside.
Pour in the coconut milk and chicken broth. Stir well.
Season with fish sauce (or soy sauce) and sugar. Adjust the seasoning to your taste.
Add Thai eggplants and sliced red bell pepper. Simmer until the chicken is cooked through and the vegetables are tender.
Taste and adjust the seasoning if needed.
Garnish with fresh basil leaves.
Serve the Green Curry Chicken over cooked jasmine rice.

Note:

- Adjust the green curry paste quantity according to your spice preference.
- You can customize the vegetables based on availability and preference. Bamboo shoots, green beans, or baby corn work well too.

Chicken Adobo:

Ingredients:

- 2 pounds chicken thighs and drumsticks, bone-in and skin-on
- 1 onion, peeled and sliced
- 1 head garlic, peeled and minced
- 1 cup soy sauce
- 1 cup white vinegar
- 1 teaspoon whole peppercorns
- 3 bay leaves
- 1 tablespoon vegetable oil
- 1 cup water
- Salt and pepper to taste
- Cooked white rice for serving

Instructions:

Marinate the Chicken:
- In a large bowl, combine chicken, sliced onions, minced garlic, soy sauce, and whole peppercorns. Massage the marinade into the chicken pieces. Marinate in the refrigerator for at least 30 minutes or preferably overnight for more flavor.

Cook the Chicken:
- Heat vegetable oil in a large, deep skillet or pot over medium heat. Remove chicken from the marinade, reserving the marinade.

Sear the Chicken:
- Sear the chicken pieces on all sides until golden brown. This step adds flavor to the dish.

Add Marinade and Simmer:
- Pour in the reserved marinade, white vinegar, and water. Add bay leaves. Bring the mixture to a boil.

Simmer:
- Reduce heat to low, cover, and let it simmer for about 30 to 40 minutes or until the chicken is tender and cooked through. Stir occasionally.

Adjust Seasoning:
- Taste and adjust the seasoning with salt and pepper. The soy sauce provides saltiness, so be cautious with additional salt.

Finish:

- Once the chicken is tender, uncover the pot and let it simmer for an additional 10-15 minutes to allow the sauce to thicken.

Serve:
- Serve the Chicken Adobo over cooked white rice. Spoon the rich sauce over the chicken pieces.

Note:

- Chicken Adobo is often enjoyed with a side of steamed white rice, but it can also be paired with potatoes, bread, or noodles.
- The longer you marinate the chicken, the more flavorful it will be. Overnight marination is ideal if time allows.
- Adjust the level of vinegar and soy sauce according to your taste preference. Some people prefer a slightly more tangy or salty Adobo.

Beef Rendang:

Ingredients:

For the Spice Paste:

- 6 shallots, peeled
- 4 cloves garlic, peeled
- 2 lemongrass stalks, white part only, thinly sliced
- 1-inch galangal, peeled and sliced
- 1-inch ginger, peeled and sliced
- 4 red chillies, deseeded
- 4 dried red chillies, soaked in hot water
- 1 tablespoon coriander powder
- 1 teaspoon cumin powder
- 1 teaspoon turmeric powder
- 1 teaspoon fennel seeds
- 1 teaspoon cinnamon powder
- 1 teaspoon ground nutmeg

For the Rendang:

- 2 pounds beef chuck or round, cut into cubes
- 2 cans (27 oz each) coconut milk
- 4 kaffir lime leaves, torn
- 2 turmeric leaves, torn (optional)
- 2 lemongrass stalks, bruised
- 2 tablespoons tamarind paste
- 2 tablespoons palm sugar or brown sugar
- Salt to taste
- 2 tablespoons vegetable oil

Instructions:

Prepare the Spice Paste:

In a blender or food processor, combine all the spice paste ingredients. Blend until you get a smooth and aromatic paste.

Make the Rendang:

Heat vegetable oil in a large pot or Dutch oven over medium heat.
Add the spice paste and sauté for 3-5 minutes until fragrant.
Add the beef cubes and cook until browned on all sides.
Pour in the coconut milk, add kaffir lime leaves, turmeric leaves (if using), lemongrass stalks, tamarind paste, and palm sugar.
Stir well and bring the mixture to a boil.
Reduce the heat to low, cover the pot, and let it simmer for about 2 to 3 hours or until the beef is tender and the sauce has thickened. Stir occasionally to prevent sticking.
Season with salt to taste.
Continue simmering until the beef is caramelized and the sauce is rich and thick.
Serve Beef Rendang with steamed rice.

Note:

- Beef Rendang is traditionally a slow-cooked dish, and the longer it cooks, the more flavorful and tender the beef becomes.
- If you can't find turmeric leaves, you can omit them, and the dish will still be delicious.
- Adjust the level of spice by adding more or fewer chillies according to your preference.

Tom Yum Goong:

Ingredients:

- 1 pound large shrimp, peeled and deveined
- 4 cups chicken or vegetable broth
- 2 stalks lemongrass, cut into 2-inch pieces and smashed
- 4 kaffir lime leaves, torn into pieces
- 3 slices galangal or ginger
- 3 Thai bird's eye chilies, smashed (adjust to taste)
- 1 medium tomato, cut into wedges
- 1 small onion, thinly sliced
- 200g (about 7 oz) mushrooms, sliced
- 2 tablespoons fish sauce
- 2 tablespoons lime juice
- 1 teaspoon sugar
- Fresh cilantro leaves for garnish
- Thai bird's eye chilies for extra heat (optional)
- Cooked jasmine rice for serving

Instructions:

In a pot, bring the chicken or vegetable broth to a boil.
Add lemongrass, kaffir lime leaves, galangal, and Thai bird's eye chilies to the boiling broth. Let it simmer for about 5-10 minutes to infuse the flavors.
Add sliced onions, mushrooms, and tomato wedges to the pot. Cook until the vegetables are slightly tender.
Stir in the peeled and deveined shrimp. Cook until the shrimp turn pink and opaque.
Season the soup with fish sauce, lime juice, and sugar. Adjust the seasoning to your taste by adding more fish sauce, lime juice, or sugar if needed.
Remove the lemongrass stalks, kaffir lime leaves, and galangal slices before serving.
Ladle the Tom Yum Goong soup into bowls.
Garnish with fresh cilantro leaves and additional Thai bird's eye chilies for those who prefer extra heat.
Serve Tom Yum Goong hot with steamed jasmine rice.

Note:

- You can customize the level of spiciness by adjusting the amount of Thai bird's eye chilies.
- Feel free to add other ingredients like straw mushrooms, baby corn, or tofu according to your preference.
- Tom Yum Goong is meant to be a hot and sour soup, so feel free to adjust the balance of lime juice and fish sauce based on your taste preference.

Laksa:

Ingredients:

For the Laksa Paste:

- 4 dried red chillies, soaked in hot water
- 2 stalks lemongrass, white part only, chopped
- 4 shallots, peeled and chopped
- 4 cloves garlic, peeled
- 1-inch piece galangal, peeled and sliced
- 1 tablespoon coriander powder
- 1 teaspoon turmeric powder
- 1 teaspoon shrimp paste (optional)
- 2 tablespoons vegetable oil

For the Laksa Soup:

- 200g (about 7 oz) rice vermicelli noodles, soaked in hot water
- 400ml (about 13.5 oz) coconut milk
- 4 cups chicken or vegetable broth
- 200g (about 7 oz) prawns, peeled and deveined
- 200g (about 7 oz) chicken breast, thinly sliced (optional)
- 2 tablespoons fish sauce
- 1 tablespoon soy sauce
- 1 tablespoon brown sugar
- Bean sprouts for garnish
- Fresh cilantro leaves for garnish
- Hard-boiled eggs, halved (optional)
- Lime wedges for serving

Instructions:

Prepare the Laksa Paste:

In a blender or food processor, combine soaked dried red chillies, lemongrass, shallots, garlic, galangal, coriander powder, turmeric powder, and shrimp paste (if using). Blend until you get a smooth paste.

Heat vegetable oil in a large pot over medium heat. Add the laksa paste and sauté for 5-7 minutes until fragrant.

Make the Laksa Soup:

Add chicken or vegetable broth to the pot with the laksa paste. Bring to a simmer.
Pour in the coconut milk, fish sauce, soy sauce, and brown sugar. Stir well.
Add prawns and sliced chicken (if using). Cook until the prawns are pink and opaque, and the chicken is cooked through.
Taste the soup and adjust the seasoning with more fish sauce or sugar if needed.
Drain the soaked rice vermicelli noodles and divide them among serving bowls.
Ladle the laksa soup over the noodles.
Garnish with bean sprouts, fresh cilantro leaves, and halved hard-boiled eggs (if using).
Serve Laksa hot with lime wedges on the side.

Note:

- Laksa is a versatile dish, and you can customize it with your choice of protein, such as tofu or seafood.
- Adjust the spice level by adding more or fewer dried red chillies in the laksa paste.
- Laksa is traditionally served with rice vermicelli noodles, but you can use other noodle varieties if preferred.

Banh Mi Sandwich:

Ingredients:

For the Grilled Protein:

- 1 pound protein of choice (pork, chicken, beef, tofu), thinly sliced
- 2 tablespoons soy sauce
- 1 tablespoon fish sauce (or soy sauce for vegetarian version)
- 1 tablespoon sugar
- 1 tablespoon vegetable oil
- 2 cloves garlic, minced
- 1 teaspoon five-spice powder (optional)

For the Pickled Vegetables:

- 1 cup julienned carrots
- 1 cup julienned daikon radish
- 1/2 cup rice vinegar
- 1/2 cup water
- 2 tablespoons sugar
- 1 teaspoon salt

For the Sriracha Mayo:

- 1/2 cup mayonnaise
- 2 tablespoons Sriracha sauce

For Assembly:

- Baguette or French bread, cut into sandwich-sized pieces
- Fresh cilantro leaves
- Fresh mint leaves
- Sliced cucumber

Instructions:

Marinate and Grill the Protein:

In a bowl, combine soy sauce, fish sauce, sugar, vegetable oil, minced garlic, and five-spice powder. Mix well.

Add the thinly sliced protein of choice to the marinade. Toss to coat evenly and let it marinate for at least 30 minutes.

Grill the marinated protein until fully cooked and slightly caramelized.

Prepare the Pickled Vegetables:

In a bowl, combine julienned carrots and daikon radish.

In a saucepan, heat rice vinegar, water, sugar, and salt until the sugar and salt dissolve. Allow the mixture to cool.

Pour the cooled vinegar mixture over the julienned vegetables. Let it marinate for at least 1 hour or overnight.

Make the Sriracha Mayo:

In a small bowl, mix mayonnaise and Sriracha sauce until well combined.

Assemble the Banh Mi Sandwich:

Slice the baguette or French bread horizontally.
Spread a generous layer of Sriracha mayo on both sides of the bread.
Arrange the grilled protein on one side of the bread.
Drain the pickled vegetables and add them on top of the protein.
Add fresh cilantro leaves, mint leaves, and sliced cucumber.
Close the sandwich and press gently.
Serve the Banh Mi Sandwich immediately and enjoy the burst of flavors.

Note:

- Feel free to customize the Banh Mi with additional toppings like sliced jalapeños or a drizzle of hoisin sauce for extra flavor.
- Traditional Banh Mi often includes pâté, but this recipe focuses on a simplified, delicious version.

Seafood Dishes:

Thai Basil Shrimp Stir-Fry:

Ingredients:

- 1 pound large shrimp, peeled and deveined
- 2 tablespoons vegetable oil
- 4 cloves garlic, minced
- 2 Thai bird's eye chilies, chopped (adjust to spice preference)
- 1 cup fresh Thai basil leaves
- 1 tablespoon fish sauce
- 1 tablespoon oyster sauce
- 1 teaspoon soy sauce
- 1 teaspoon sugar
- Freshly ground black pepper, to taste

Instructions:

Prepare Shrimp:
- Pat the shrimp dry with paper towels. If they are large, you can cut them in half lengthwise.

Heat Oil:
- Heat vegetable oil in a wok or a large skillet over medium-high heat.

Sauté Garlic and Chilies:
- Add minced garlic and chopped Thai bird's eye chilies to the hot oil. Sauté for about 30 seconds or until fragrant.

Add Shrimp:
- Add the shrimp to the wok and stir-fry for 2-3 minutes until they start to turn pink.

Season with Sauces:
- In a small bowl, mix together fish sauce, oyster sauce, soy sauce, and sugar. Pour the sauce over the shrimp and stir well to coat.

Add Basil:
- Add fresh Thai basil leaves to the wok and toss until the basil wilts and the shrimp are fully cooked.

Season with Pepper:
- Season the stir-fry with freshly ground black pepper to taste.

Serve:
- Serve the Thai Basil Shrimp Stir-Fry hot over steamed jasmine rice.

Enjoy the vibrant and aromatic flavors of this Thai Basil Shrimp Stir-Fry. The combination of garlic, Thai basil, and chilies adds a burst of flavor to the succulent shrimp. It's a quick and delicious seafood dish that pairs perfectly with steamed rice.

Indonesian Grilled Fish (Ikan Bakar):

Ingredients:

For Spice Paste (Bumbu:

- 5 shallots, peeled
- 3 cloves garlic, peeled
- 2 red bird's eye chilies (adjust to spice preference)
- 2 candlenuts or macadamia nuts
- 1 inch galangal, peeled and sliced
- 1 lemongrass stalk, white part only, sliced
- 1 teaspoon turmeric powder or 1 small turmeric root, peeled
- 1 teaspoon tamarind paste
- 1 tablespoon palm sugar or brown sugar
- 1 teaspoon salt

For Grilled Fish:

- 2 whole fish (snapper or mackerel), cleaned and scaled
- Banana leaves or aluminum foil (for wrapping)
- Lime wedges (for serving)

Instructions:

For Spice Paste:

Blend Spice Paste:
- In a blender or food processor, blend shallots, garlic, red chilies, candlenuts, galangal, lemongrass, turmeric, tamarind paste, palm sugar, and salt until you get a smooth paste.

For Grilled Fish:

Prepare Fish:
- Clean and scale the whole fish. Make a few diagonal cuts on each side of the fish to allow the marinade to penetrate.

Marinate Fish:
- Rub the spice paste all over the fish, making sure to get it into the cuts. Allow the fish to marinate for at least 30 minutes to an hour.

Wrap in Banana Leaves:
- If using banana leaves, wrap each fish in a banana leaf, securing it with toothpicks. If using aluminum foil, wrap the fish securely.

Grill:
- Preheat a grill or barbecue. Grill the fish over medium-high heat for about 15-20 minutes, turning halfway through, until the fish is cooked and has a nice char.

Serve:
- Unwrap the grilled fish and serve hot with lime wedges on the side.

Enjoy the delightful flavors of Indonesian Grilled Fish (Ikan Bakar). The aromatic spice paste infuses the fish with a rich and savory taste, complemented by the smokiness from the grill. Serve it with steamed rice or your favorite side dishes for a complete and satisfying meal.

Burmese Mohinga (Fish Soup):

Ingredients:

For the Broth:

- 1 pound white fish fillets (catfish or any white fish)
- 1 onion, sliced
- 4 cloves garlic, minced
- 2 lemongrass stalks, bruised
- 1-inch piece of ginger, sliced
- 1 tablespoon fish sauce
- 1 teaspoon turmeric powder
- 1 teaspoon paprika
- 1 teaspoon chili powder (adjust to spice preference)
- 6 cups fish or chicken stock
- Salt to taste

Other Ingredients:

- 250g thin rice noodles, cooked according to package instructions
- Fish sauce, to taste
- 2 tablespoons vegetable oil
- 1 onion, thinly sliced
- 4 cloves garlic, minced
- 1 teaspoon ground coriander
- 1 teaspoon ground cumin
- Toppings: Hard-boiled eggs, chopped cilantro, lime wedges, sliced green onions, crispy fried onions, and fresh cilantro.

Instructions:

For the Broth:

    Prepare Fish Fillets:
- Rinse the fish fillets and pat them dry. Season with salt.

    Make Broth:
- In a large pot, combine fish fillets, sliced onion, minced garlic, lemongrass stalks, sliced ginger, fish sauce, turmeric powder, paprika, chili powder, and

fish or chicken stock. Bring to a simmer and let it cook for about 20-25 minutes.

Strain Broth:
- Strain the broth to remove solids, leaving a clear and flavorful liquid.

Other Ingredients:

Prepare Rice Noodles:
- Cook the rice noodles according to the package instructions. Drain and set aside.

Sauté Aromatics:
- In a separate pan, heat vegetable oil over medium heat. Sauté sliced onion until caramelized. Add minced garlic and continue to sauté until fragrant. Add ground coriander and ground cumin, stirring for another minute.

Combine Broth and Aromatics:
- Pour the strained broth into the pan with sautéed aromatics. Allow it to simmer for an additional 10-15 minutes.

Adjust Seasoning:
- Season the broth with fish sauce to taste.

Assemble Mohinga:
- To serve, place a portion of cooked rice noodles in a bowl. Ladle the hot broth over the noodles.

Add Toppings:
- Garnish with hard-boiled eggs, chopped cilantro, lime wedges, sliced green onions, crispy fried onions, and fresh cilantro.

Serve Hot:
- Serve the Burmese Mohinga hot, allowing each person to customize their toppings.

Enjoy the comforting and flavorful Burmese Mohinga, a fish-based soup with rice noodles that brings together a harmonious blend of aromatic spices and fresh toppings.

Vegetarian Delights:

Indian Vegetable Biryani:

Ingredients:

For Rice:

- 2 cups basmati rice, soaked for 30 minutes and drained
- 4 cups water
- 1 bay leaf
- 2-3 green cardamom pods
- 2-3 cloves
- 1-inch cinnamon stick
- Salt to taste

For Vegetable Layer:

- 2 tablespoons ghee or vegetable oil
- 1 large onion, thinly sliced
- 1 cup mixed vegetables (carrots, peas, beans, potatoes), chopped
- 1 cup cauliflower florets
- 1/2 cup yogurt
- 1 teaspoon ginger-garlic paste
- 1/2 teaspoon turmeric powder
- 1 teaspoon red chili powder (adjust to spice preference)
- 1 teaspoon biryani masala
- Salt to taste
- Fresh coriander leaves and mint leaves for garnish

For Biryani Masala:

- 1 black cardamom pod
- 4-5 green cardamom pods
- 4 cloves
- 1-inch cinnamon stick

- 1 teaspoon fennel seeds
- 1 teaspoon cumin seeds

Instructions:

For Rice:

Cook Rice:
- In a large pot, bring water to a boil. Add soaked and drained basmati rice, bay leaf, green cardamom pods, cloves, cinnamon stick, and salt. Cook until the rice is 70% cooked. Drain the water and set aside.

For Vegetable Layer:

Prepare Biryani Masala:
- In a small pan, dry roast black cardamom, green cardamom pods, cloves, cinnamon stick, fennel seeds, and cumin seeds. Grind them into a fine powder to make the biryani masala.

Sauté Onions:
- In a large skillet or pot, heat ghee or vegetable oil over medium heat. Add thinly sliced onions and sauté until golden brown.

Cook Vegetables:
- Add mixed vegetables and cauliflower florets to the skillet. Sauté for a few minutes until they start to soften.

Add Yogurt and Spices:
- Stir in yogurt, ginger-garlic paste, turmeric powder, red chili powder, biryani masala, and salt. Cook until the vegetables are coated with the spices and the yogurt is well incorporated.

Layering:
- In the same pot used for cooking rice, layer half of the partially cooked rice. Top it with the prepared vegetable mixture. Sprinkle fresh coriander leaves and mint leaves. Add the remaining rice as the top layer.

Dum Cooking:
- Cover the pot with a tight-fitting lid or seal it with aluminum foil. Cook on low heat for 20-25 minutes. This process is known as dum cooking.

Serve:
- Once done, gently fluff the biryani with a fork. Serve hot, garnished with more fresh coriander and mint leaves.

Enjoy the aromatic and flavorful Indian Vegetable Biryani, a classic dish that brings together fragrant basmati rice, mixed vegetables, and a blend of aromatic spices. This vegetarian delight is perfect for a hearty and satisfying meal.

Thai Green Papaya Salad (Som Tum):

Ingredients:

- 1 medium-sized green papaya, peeled and shredded
- 2-3 cherry tomatoes, halved
- 2-3 Thai bird's eye chilies, finely chopped (adjust to spice preference)
- 2 cloves garlic, minced
- 1-2 tablespoons fish sauce (adjust to taste)
- 1-2 tablespoons palm sugar or brown sugar (adjust to taste)
- Juice of 2 limes
- 2 tablespoons roasted peanuts, crushed
- 1 tablespoon dried shrimp (optional)
- Long beans, cut into 2-inch pieces (optional)
- Cherry tomatoes, halved (optional)
- Cabbage leaves for serving

Instructions:

Prepare Green Papaya:
- Peel the green papaya and shred it using a grater or a julienne peeler. Place the shredded papaya in a large mixing bowl.

Make Dressing:
- In a small bowl, mix together chopped Thai bird's eye chilies, minced garlic, fish sauce, palm sugar, and lime juice. Adjust the quantities to achieve a balance of sweet, salty, and sour flavors.

Combine Ingredients:
- Add the halved cherry tomatoes to the shredded papaya. Pour the dressing over the papaya and tomatoes. Toss everything together to coat the papaya evenly with the dressing.

Add Peanuts and Dried Shrimp:
- Sprinkle crushed roasted peanuts and dried shrimp over the salad. Toss again to combine.

Adjust Seasoning:
- Taste the salad and adjust the seasoning if needed. Add more fish sauce, sugar, or lime juice according to your preference.

Optional Additions:

- If desired, add long beans and additional halved cherry tomatoes for extra texture and flavor.

Serve:
- To serve, line a plate with cabbage leaves and pile the Thai Green Papaya Salad on top. Garnish with extra peanuts and lime wedges if desired.

Enjoy the refreshing and vibrant flavors of Thai Green Papaya Salad (Som Tum). This dish is a delightful combination of crisp green papaya, zesty lime, spicy chilies, and the umami goodness of fish sauce, creating a perfect balance of flavors that make it a popular Thai street food favorite.

Vietnamese Vegan Pho Chay:

Ingredients:

For the Broth:

- 1 large onion, halved
- 1 large ginger piece, sliced
- 4-5 star anise
- 4-5 whole cloves
- 1 cinnamon stick
- 1 cardamom pod
- 1 tablespoon coriander seeds
- 1 large carrot, chopped
- 4-5 dried shiitake mushrooms
- 8 cups vegetable broth
- 2 tablespoons soy sauce or tamari
- 1 tablespoon coconut sugar or brown sugar
- Salt, to taste

For the Pho:

- Rice noodles, cooked according to package instructions
- Tofu, sliced and pan-fried
- Bean sprouts
- Fresh herbs (cilantro, mint, Thai basil)
- Lime wedges
- Red chili, sliced
- Hoisin sauce and Sriracha (optional, for serving)

Instructions:

For the Broth:

    Char Onion and Ginger:

- Place onion halves and ginger slices on a baking sheet. Broil or char them over an open flame until they get a nice char on the edges.

Toast Spices:
- In a dry pot, toast star anise, cloves, cinnamon stick, cardamom pod, and coriander seeds until fragrant.

Simmer Broth:
- Add the charred onion and ginger, chopped carrot, dried shiitake mushrooms, vegetable broth, soy sauce or tamari, and coconut sugar to the pot. Bring to a boil, then reduce heat and simmer for at least 30 minutes to allow the flavors to infuse. Season with salt to taste.

Strain Broth:
- Strain the broth to remove solids, leaving a clear and flavorful liquid.

For the Pho:

Prepare Rice Noodles:
- Cook rice noodles according to package instructions. Drain and set aside.

Pan-fry Tofu:
- Slice tofu and pan-fry until golden brown on each side.

Assemble Pho:
- In serving bowls, place a portion of cooked rice noodles and arrange tofu slices on top.

Pour Hot Broth:
- Pour hot broth over the noodles and tofu. The hot broth will heat up the tofu.

Garnish:
- Garnish the pho with bean sprouts, fresh herbs (cilantro, mint, Thai basil), lime wedges, and sliced red chili.

Serve:
- Serve Vietnamese Vegan Pho Chay hot, with hoisin sauce and Sriracha on the side for those who like extra flavor.

Enjoy the comforting and aromatic flavors of Vietnamese Vegan Pho Chay, a plant-based version of the classic Vietnamese pho. This nourishing and flavorful soup is perfect for a cozy and satisfying meal.

Side Dishes:

Indonesian Gado Gado:

Ingredients:

For the Peanut Sauce:

- 1 cup unsalted roasted peanuts
- 3 cloves garlic, minced
- 2 tablespoons palm sugar or brown sugar
- 1 tablespoon tamarind paste
- 2 tablespoons sweet soy sauce (kecap manis)
- 1 teaspoon sambal or chili paste (adjust to spice preference)
- 1/2 cup coconut milk
- Salt, to taste
- Water, as needed to adjust consistency

For the Salad:

- Cabbage, thinly sliced
- Bean sprouts
- Long beans, cut into 2-inch pieces and blanched
- Carrots, julienned and blanched
- Potatoes, boiled and sliced
- Tofu, fried or pan-fried
- Hard-boiled eggs, halved
- Cucumber, sliced

Instructions:

For the Peanut Sauce:

Blend Peanuts:
- In a blender or food processor, blend roasted peanuts until you get a coarse powder.

Prepare Peanut Sauce:

- In a saucepan, combine minced garlic, palm sugar, tamarind paste, sweet soy sauce, chili paste, and coconut milk. Heat over medium heat, stirring until the sugar is dissolved.

Add Peanut Powder:
- Add the blended peanuts to the saucepan and mix well. If the sauce is too thick, add water gradually until you achieve the desired consistency.

Season:
- Season the peanut sauce with salt to taste. Let it simmer for a few minutes until it thickens slightly. Remove from heat and set aside.

For the Salad:

Prepare Vegetables:
- Prepare all the vegetables by slicing, julienned, or blanching them as needed.

Assemble Salad:
- Arrange the sliced cabbage, bean sprouts, long beans, julienned carrots, boiled potatoes, fried tofu, hard-boiled eggs, and cucumber on a serving plate.

Drizzle Peanut Sauce:
- Drizzle the prepared peanut sauce over the vegetables.

Serve:
- Serve Indonesian Gado Gado immediately, allowing everyone to mix the vegetables and sauce together.

Enjoy the delightful mix of textures and flavors in Indonesian Gado Gado, a vibrant mixed vegetable salad with a rich and flavorful peanut sauce dressing. This dish is not only delicious but also a feast for the eyes with its colorful array of fresh vegetables.

Cambodian Pickled Vegetables (Tuk Meric):

Ingredients:

For Pickling Liquid:

- 1 cup rice vinegar
- 1 cup water
- 1/2 cup sugar
- 1 tablespoon salt

For Pickled Vegetables:

- 1 large cucumber, thinly sliced
- 1 medium carrot, julienned
- 1 small daikon radish, julienned
- 1 red bell pepper, thinly sliced
- 2-3 cloves garlic, minced
- 2-3 red bird's eye chilies, finely chopped (adjust to spice preference)
- 1 tablespoon chopped cilantro (optional)

Instructions:

Prepare Pickling Liquid:
- In a small saucepan, combine rice vinegar, water, sugar, and salt. Heat over medium heat, stirring until the sugar and salt dissolve. Bring to a simmer, then remove from heat and let it cool.

Prepare Vegetables:
- Wash and prepare the vegetables. Thinly slice the cucumber, julienne the carrot and daikon radish, and thinly slice the red bell pepper.

Combine Vegetables:
- In a large bowl, combine the sliced cucumber, julienned carrot, daikon radish, red bell pepper, minced garlic, chopped cilantro (if using), and chopped bird's eye chilies.

Pour Pickling Liquid:
- Pour the cooled pickling liquid over the vegetables. Ensure that the liquid covers all the vegetables.

Mix Well:
- Gently toss the vegetables in the pickling liquid to ensure even coating.

Marinate:
- Cover the bowl and let the vegetables marinate in the pickling liquid for at least 1-2 hours, or overnight for more intense flavors.

Serve:
- Once marinated, Cambodian Pickled Vegetables (Tuk Meric) are ready to be served. You can serve them as a tangy and spicy side dish or as a refreshing accompaniment to main dishes.

Enjoy the tangy and spicy flavors of Cambodian Pickled Vegetables (Tuk Meric) as a delightful side dish. The combination of crunchy vegetables and the zesty pickling liquid creates a refreshing and vibrant addition to your meal.

Desserts:

Thai Mango Sticky Rice (Khao Niew Mamuang):

Ingredients:

- 1 cup glutinous rice
- 1 cup coconut milk
- 1/2 cup sugar
- 1/2 teaspoon salt
- 2 ripe mangoes, peeled and sliced
- Sesame seeds for garnish (optional)

Instructions:

Rinse and Soak Rice:
- Rinse the glutinous rice under cold water until the water runs clear. Soak the rice in water for at least 4 hours or preferably overnight.

Steam Rice:
- Drain the soaked rice. Place it in a steamer lined with cheesecloth or muslin cloth. Steam the rice over medium-high heat for 25-30 minutes or until it becomes translucent and sticky.

Prepare Coconut Sauce:
- In a saucepan, combine coconut milk, sugar, and salt. Heat over medium heat, stirring until the sugar and salt dissolve. Once the rice is cooked, pour half of the coconut sauce over the rice. Let it sit for a few minutes to absorb the flavors.

Assemble Mango Sticky Rice:
- Arrange a portion of the sticky rice on a serving plate. Place mango slices on top of the rice.

Drizzle Coconut Sauce:
- Drizzle the remaining coconut sauce over the mango and rice. You can also garnish with sesame seeds for added texture and flavor.

Serve:
- Serve Thai Mango Sticky Rice (Khao Niew Mamuang) warm or at room temperature. Enjoy the delightful combination of sweet sticky rice, juicy mango slices, and rich coconut sauce.

Experience the heavenly flavors of Thai Mango Sticky Rice, a popular and delectable dessert that combines the sweetness of ripe mangoes, the stickiness of glutinous rice, and the richness of coconut milk. It's a delightful treat that captures the essence of Thai culinary delights.

Malaysian Kuih Dadar (Pandan Crepes):

Ingredients:

For Pandan Crepes:

- 1 cup all-purpose flour
- 1 cup coconut milk
- 1/2 cup pandan juice (blend pandan leaves with water and strain)
- 2 eggs
- 1/4 teaspoon salt
- Pandan essence (optional, for extra flavor and color)

For Filling:

- 1 cup grated coconut
- 1/2 cup palm sugar (gula melaka), grated
- 1/4 teaspoon salt

Instructions:

For Pandan Crepes:

    Prepare Batter:
- In a bowl, whisk together all-purpose flour, coconut milk, pandan juice, eggs, and salt until you get a smooth batter. Add pandan essence if desired for extra flavor and color.

    Cook Crepes:
- Heat a non-stick pan over medium heat. Pour a small ladle of batter into the pan, swirling to coat the bottom evenly. Cook until the edges start to lift, then flip and cook the other side. Repeat until all the batter is used.

    Make Pandan Crepes:
- Stack the cooked crepes on a plate. They should have a vibrant green color from the pandan juice.

For Filling:

Prepare Coconut Filling:
- In a pan, combine grated coconut, palm sugar, and salt. Cook over medium heat, stirring continuously until the sugar melts and the mixture becomes fragrant.

Assemble Kuih Dadar:
- Place a pandan crepe on a flat surface. Spoon a portion of the coconut filling along one edge of the crepe. Roll the crepe tightly to encase the filling. Repeat with the remaining crepes and filling.

Serve:
- Once assembled, slice the Malaysian Kuih Dadar into bite-sized pieces. Serve and enjoy this delightful pandan-flavored treat!

Note:

- You can also steam the crepes for a softer texture. Steam each crepe for about 1-2 minutes before adding the filling.
- Adjust the sweetness of the coconut filling according to your taste preference.

Optional Garnish:

- Sprinkle toasted sesame seeds on top for added flavor and texture.

Experience the delightful flavors of Malaysian Kuih Dadar, where pandan-flavored crepes meet a sweet coconut and palm sugar filling. This vibrant and aromatic dessert is a favorite in Malaysian cuisine, offering a perfect blend of sweetness and pandan-infused goodness.

Filipino Halo-Halo:

Ingredients:

For the Shaved Ice:

- Crushed or shaved ice

For the Halo-Halo Ingredients:

- 1/2 cup cooked sweetened red beans
- 1/2 cup cooked sweetened white beans
- 1/2 cup cooked sweetened chickpeas
- 1/2 cup sweetened jackfruit strips
- 1/2 cup sweetened macapuno (coconut sport strips)
- 1/2 cup sweetened saba bananas (plantains), sliced
- 1/2 cup nata de coco (coconut jelly cubes)
- 1/2 cup kaong (sugar palm fruit)
- 1/2 cup sweetened purple yam (ube), diced
- 1/2 cup sweetened leche flan (caramel custard), sliced into cubes
- 1/2 cup sweetened corn kernels
- Evaporated milk, to taste
- Ube (purple yam) ice cream (optional)
- Leche flan or ube jam for topping (optional)
- Shredded coconut (niyog), toasted until golden (optional)

Instructions:

   Prepare the Ingredients:
   - Cook the sweetened red beans, white beans, chickpeas, saba bananas, purple yam, and leche flan separately. Ensure they are sweetened to taste.

   Assemble Halo-Halo:
   - In a tall glass or bowl, layer the shaved ice followed by the cooked sweetened beans, fruits, and other ingredients.

   Drizzle Evaporated Milk:
   - Generously drizzle evaporated milk over the layered ingredients. You can adjust the amount based on your preference.

Top with Leche Flan or Ube Jam (Optional):
- If desired, top the halo-halo with additional slices of leche flan or a dollop of ube jam for extra richness.

Add Ube Ice Cream (Optional):
- Place a scoop of ube (purple yam) ice cream on top of the halo-halo for a delightful frozen treat.

Garnish with Toasted Shredded Coconut (Optional):
- For added texture and flavor, sprinkle toasted shredded coconut on top.

Serve and Mix:
- Serve the Filipino Halo-Halo immediately. Use a long spoon and mix the ingredients thoroughly to enjoy the delightful combination of flavors and textures.

Enjoy the refreshing and colorful Filipino Halo-Halo, a beloved dessert that captures the essence of tropical indulgence. This delightful concoction of shaved ice, sweetened fruits, and beans is perfect for cooling down on a warm day or satisfying your sweet cravings.

Vietnamese Coffee Ice Cream:

Ingredients:

For the Coffee Custard:

- 1 cup strong brewed Vietnamese coffee, cooled
- 1 cup heavy cream
- 1 cup whole milk
- 3/4 cup granulated sugar
- 5 large egg yolks

For the Coffee Swirl:

- 2 tablespoons sweetened condensed milk
- 2 tablespoons brewed Vietnamese coffee, cooled

Instructions:

Prepare the Coffee Custard:

In a saucepan, combine heavy cream, whole milk, and granulated sugar. Heat over medium heat until it reaches a gentle simmer, stirring to dissolve the sugar. In a separate bowl, whisk the egg yolks. Slowly pour the hot milk mixture into the egg yolks, whisking constantly.
Return the mixture to the saucepan and cook over low heat, stirring continuously, until it thickens and coats the back of a spoon. Do not let it boil.
Remove from heat and strain the custard into a bowl. Let it cool to room temperature, then refrigerate for at least 4 hours or overnight.

Make the Coffee Swirl:

In a small bowl, mix sweetened condensed milk with brewed Vietnamese coffee.

Churn the Ice Cream:

Pour the chilled coffee custard into an ice cream maker and churn according to the manufacturer's instructions.
Once the ice cream is almost set, drizzle the coffee swirl mixture into the churned ice cream. Continue churning until well combined.

Transfer the ice cream to a lidded container and freeze for a few hours until firm.

Serve:

Scoop the Vietnamese Coffee Ice Cream into bowls or cones.
Optionally, garnish with a sprinkle of crushed roasted peanuts or a drizzle of sweetened condensed milk.

Note:

- Vietnamese Coffee Ice Cream captures the rich and bold flavors of traditional Vietnamese coffee in a delightful frozen treat. Adjust the sweetness and coffee intensity according to your preference.

Beverages:

Vietnamese Iced Coffee (Ca Phe Sua Da):

Ingredients:

- 2 tablespoons coarsely ground Vietnamese coffee (Robusta beans)
- 4 tablespoons sweetened condensed milk
- Ice cubes

Equipment:

- Vietnamese drip filter (phin)
- Tall glass

Instructions:

Prepare Vietnamese Drip Coffee:
- Place the Vietnamese drip filter (phin) over the glass. Add coarsely ground Vietnamese coffee to the filter, leveling it out but not pressing it down too hard.

Compact Coffee:
- Use the press to compact the coffee grounds slightly. This helps in creating a strong and flavorful brew.

Brew Coffee:
- Pour a small amount of hot water (just enough to wet the coffee grounds) and let it sit for about 20-30 seconds. This allows the coffee grounds to bloom.

Add More Water:
- Fill the filter chamber with hot water up to the top. Place the lid on top to retain heat. Let the coffee drip through the filter slowly. This process may take about 5 minutes.

Mix with Condensed Milk:
- While the coffee is brewing, add sweetened condensed milk to the bottom of a glass.

Pour Brewed Coffee:
- Once the coffee has finished dripping, pour it over the condensed milk. Stir well to combine the coffee and condensed milk.

Add Ice:

- Add ice cubes to the glass to cool down the coffee and create a refreshing iced beverage.

Serve:
- Vietnamese Iced Coffee (Ca Phe Sua Da) is ready to be served. Enjoy the bold and sweet flavors of this traditional Vietnamese coffee.

Note:

- Adjust the amount of condensed milk according to your sweetness preference.
- Use Robusta coffee beans for an authentic Vietnamese coffee flavor.

Indulge in the rich and sweet experience of Vietnamese Iced Coffee (Ca Phe Sua Da). This iconic beverage, with its strong coffee and creamy condensed milk over ice, is not just a drink but a cultural delight that captures the essence of Vietnamese coffee culture.

Thai Iced Tea (Cha Yen):

Ingredients:

- 2 tablespoons Thai tea leaves
- 1 cup boiling water
- 2-3 tablespoons sweetened condensed milk (adjust to taste)
- Ice cubes

Optional:

- Evaporated milk or half-and-half for added creaminess
- Sugar, to taste

Instructions:

Brew Thai Tea:
- Place the Thai tea leaves in a heatproof container. Pour boiling water over the tea leaves and let it steep for 5-10 minutes.

Strain Tea:
- Strain the brewed tea using a fine mesh sieve or a tea strainer to remove the tea leaves.

Sweeten with Condensed Milk:
- Add sweetened condensed milk to the brewed Thai tea. Start with 2-3 tablespoons, and adjust according to your sweetness preference.

Optional: Add Sugar (To Taste):
- If desired, you can add additional sugar to the tea for extra sweetness. Stir until the sugar is completely dissolved.

Cool the Tea:
- Let the sweetened Thai tea cool to room temperature. You can speed up the process by placing it in the refrigerator.

Serve Over Ice:
- Fill glasses with ice cubes and pour the sweetened Thai tea over the ice.

Optional: Add Evaporated Milk or Half-and-Half:
- For added creaminess, you can top the Thai iced tea with a splash of evaporated milk or half-and-half. Stir gently to mix.

Serve and Enjoy:
- Thai Iced Tea (Cha Yen) is ready to be enjoyed. Sip on this sweet and creamy beverage to cool down on a hot day.

Note:

- Thai tea leaves are specifically blended for making Thai iced tea and can be found in Asian grocery stores.
- Adjust the sweetness and creaminess to suit your taste preferences.

Savor the delightful flavors of Thai Iced Tea (Cha Yen), a sweet and creamy beverage that perfectly balances the boldness of Thai tea with the richness of condensed milk. Whether enjoyed on its own or paired with your favorite Thai dishes, this refreshing drink is a true Thai culinary experience.

Indonesian Avocado Shake (Es Alpukat):

Ingredients:

- 2 ripe avocados, peeled and pitted
- 2 tablespoons sweetened condensed milk (adjust to taste)
- 1 cup ice cubes
- 1/2 cup milk (whole milk or condensed milk for a richer taste)
- Chocolate syrup (optional, for garnish)

Instructions:

Prepare Avocados:
- Scoop out the flesh of the ripe avocados and place it in a blender.

Add Condensed Milk:
- Add sweetened condensed milk to the blender. Start with 2 tablespoons and adjust according to your sweetness preference.

Blend:
- Blend the avocados and condensed milk until smooth and creamy. If the mixture is too thick, you can add a little milk to help with blending.

Add Ice Cubes:
- Add ice cubes to the blender to create a refreshing and chilled shake.

Pour Milk:
- Pour milk into the blender. Use whole milk for a creamy texture or condensed milk for a richer flavor.

Blend Until Smooth:
- Blend all the ingredients until smooth and well combined. Check the consistency and add more milk if needed.

Optional: Drizzle Chocolate Syrup:
- If desired, drizzle chocolate syrup on the inside of serving glasses before pouring the avocado shake for an extra touch of sweetness and decoration.

Serve:
- Pour the Indonesian Avocado Shake (Es Alpukat) into glasses and serve immediately. Enjoy the creamy and sweet goodness of this delightful shake.

Note:

- Adjust the sweetness by adding more or less condensed milk according to your taste.
- You can also add a scoop of vanilla ice cream for an indulgent treat.

Indulge in the creamy and sweet delight of Indonesian Avocado Shake (Es Alpukat). This refreshing beverage combines the natural creaminess of ripe avocados with the sweetness of condensed milk, creating a perfect treat for a hot day or as a sweet ending to your meal.

www.ingramcontent.com/pod-product-compliance
Lightning Source LLC
LaVergne TN
LVHW062048070526
838201LV00080B/2261